ABRACADABRA!

Improve the Place Where You Work

Zelma Lansford, Ed.D.

www.zelmalansford.com

Ⓢpiral Publications

Atlanta, Georgia

Second Printing

Printed in the United States of America

ISBN 978-0-9821833-0-4

Table of Contents

For all the "Suzies" and "Georges" in the Workplace and with thanks to Victoria and Skyler who are my inspiration.

The Quick Fix

Have you ever wished you could wave a magic wand over your workplace and instantly make your job more enjoyable? Perhaps you feel like the young man I encountered while walking through the lobby of a technology client. Jeff, a twenty-something, greeted me with a warm handshake and asked where I was going. I replied that I was on my way to a session with some of his senior managers. "Dr. Z," he said, "Could you tell them something that will make it easier for me to do my best every day so that I don't have to dread coming to work?" I smiled and assured him that we were working on his concern. His was a familiar issue that I often hear when beginning work with a new company.

Sometimes, supervisors don't hear the difference between a self-centered gripe and a concern about what's interfering with an employee's best performance.

Why would any organization make it difficult for an employee as bright and capable as Jeff? Why would anyone who was so excited about what he was working on dread coming to work? What were the barriers that Jeff's organization was creating? The easy answer most employers assume is that the problem is Jeff's. It's always easier to blame the individual than to probe the organizational structure, improve the process, or fix the problem.

If his organization replaced Jeff with someone who was equally competent but with a better attitude, would the situation improve? It's unlikely, because Jeff didn't have a bad attitude, he was just expressing frustration over not being able to do his best work every day. Is that so bad? Well, in some organizations, openly expressing dissatisfaction of any kind is verboten. Sometimes, supervisors don't hear the difference between a self-centered gripe and a concern about what's interfering with an employee's best performance. The result is to blame the employee or minimize the legitimacy of the concern. Managers can become defensive and try to rationalize away concerns that need to be addressed.

The reason that magic is needed to fix a situation like Jeff's is that it's easy to overlook a fundamental principle of organizational success—organizations begin with individuals. There's a connection between what is beneficial for both. When we solve problems and remove barriers to individual performance, we unleash all kinds of improvements for the organization.

The challenge is in persuading people to see how easy it is to accept the small changes that produce major results. We frequently assume that complex organizations require complex lengthy solutions and overlook some basics. In the two decades that I've worked as an individual and organization development specialist, I've learned that there are three practices common to making many kinds of organizations function better. Whether public or private, billion dollar corporations or small businesses, in government or institutions, and from Massachusetts to California, I've found the same essentials. Although these three changes don't cover cash flow, inventory turns, lean processes, six sigma, or other efficiency measures, the three keys are the catalysts that unlock many other useful moves and practices, enabling them to become part of the organization's foundation and produce increased effectiveness and profits. These areas, if improved, can significantly change the whole work environment and enhance success, even though each organization's focus and fundamental issues may be radically dissimilar. When the improvements are initiated by top leadership, the results are truly magical, but anyone can initiate the process and make a sensational difference at any level.

The quick fix can happen, not because "one size fits all," but because there are three basic practices that can be the beginning of any organization's long-term success.

The Magical Conversation

Recently, during the drive to an off-site session with a client, I was again confronted by the same themes, but this time, the CEO gave me a unique opportunity to demonstrate exactly how easy the solution can be. The CEO had invited me to ride with him, using the time to probe for information and insights that I had developed regarding the company. He asked about the feedback from employees and how his managers compared to those in other businesses. I diplomatically answered his questions, but sensed that he wanted more. Then, he said, "If you could wave a magic wand over our company and make it instantly better, the preferred workplace in the region, and increase our profits, what would you change?"

. . . value the people as assets in the same way that the equipment, real estate, and other concrete assets are valued.

I told him that there were many areas that could be enhanced, but three simple changes could produce significant improvements in job satisfaction for employees, and at the same time, lay the foundation to build a more profitable and successful business.

"You think it's that simple? Just how much magic is involved?" he said with a smirk.

"Well, defining the three areas is very simple and implementing the improvements will be low cost, but taking ownership of the changes will require considerable commitment from everyone. That's the part that may need a magic wand and lots of pixie dust," I responded.

"You've got my curiosity," he said with a skeptical smile.

The First Wish: Value the People

"What I would wish for is simply that everyone in the company would value the people as assets in the same way that the equipment, real estate, and other concrete assets are valued. I know that you want everyone in your organization to be treated with respect, talked to as adults, and regarded with trust. The reality is that most of the policies and rules treat people, especially the hourly employees, as fifth graders. Everyone seems to be monitored as if they were the enemy. With all of those policies in place, the managers come along and bark orders in a very condescending tone and people don't feel valued."

"Surely, it's not that bad," interrupted the CEO.

"Look, I know that this is not an easy topic. Are you sure you want me to continue?" I asked.

"Well, yes, it's not that I don't believe you," he said. "It's just that 'we treat our people like fifth graders' is hard to hear."

"I'm willing to be wrong," I replied. "In fact, I love being wrong about these kinds of issues. But, I've spent

Communications often reflect
needs for power rather than
clear, concise information and
problem solving.

considerable time in your different locations facilitating the feedback sessions in all departments, on different shifts, and talking with lots of individual employees. I *really* believe there's an opportunity here." I insisted.

"You're right. I guess I'm just being defensive, but 'fifth graders,' isn't that's an exaggeration?" he chided.

"Perhaps, but I'll let you decide after I give you some examples," I responded. "Last Wednesday evening, I met with hourly employees on the 3:00 to 11:00 p.m. shift in your Greenville Plant. As I began the introductions, one of the employees told me that Suzie would be late because she was talking with the supervisor. I thanked the man and continued. Shortly, Suzie, a woman in her fifties with gray hair and a scowl walked into the room and flopped into a chair. I welcomed her and began to proceed when she interrupted, 'You probably don't want me here. You don't want my opinion about what it's like to work here —not today!'"

I reassured her and asked, "Did something happen today?" Then, she began to tell me a story about how, since business had been slow, her shift had only been working four days each week for the past five months. She said that when she arrived that day, the supervisor had greeted her with the words, "You're working Friday!"

"He said it just like that?" I asked her.

Suzie replied, "Yeah, no smile, nothing friendly, just the command, 'You're working Friday!'" Then she continued with, "Now, after having a four-day paycheck for three months, I'd ordinarily jump at the chance for more work."

She talked about liking her job, having worked at the plant for 24 years, and needing the money. Her problem was that she had promised to take her grandchildren on a picnic and to the amusement park on Friday. If she'd been given some advance notice, she said that she could have changed her plans, but at the last minute, it was difficult to tell four little kids that it couldn't happen when they had been looking forward to it for weeks. She told the supervisor that, since they had only been working four days each week that she had made plans for Friday. Suzie said that the supervisor just glared at her and told her that he had a special order on her machine and it had to run. Then he barked, "As I said, you're working Friday!" and walked away.

As the tears welled-up in Suzie's eyes, the lady sitting next to her said, "Suzie, I can run your machine. It's like mine. I need work. I'll work in your place on Friday."

I interrupted and said, "That's a great idea. You two can talk to the supervisor after we finish here. I'm sure that you can work something out."

I turned to the CEO and said, "You see, this is just one of countless examples of how the supervisor exercised his power and unnecessarily demoralized an employee by using poor communications. If he had only pleasantly said, 'Suzie, there's a special order that needs to run on your machine on Friday, would you like to work?' Then, Suzie could have regrettably declined with dignity and the supervisor could have moved on to the next person on the seniority list who would likely have jumped at the chance for a full pay-check."

The CEO asked, "Are you telling me that this sort of thing happens often?"

"Frequently," I replied.

"But only with the supervisors and hourly people, right?"

"No, at every level," I reminded him. "Remember that exchange between two of the senior managers during that meeting last week? Their communications also reflect needs for power rather than clear, concise information and problem solving. You'll recall that Will and Chuck had discovered some delays in customer deliveries. Instead of going to George, presenting the situation, and asking what was needed to solve the problem, Will and Chuck attacked George in the meeting. They succeeded in putting George on the defensive, making him look bad in front of you, and escalating the whole problem when you became involved. The way that people communicate is the key to building trust and a culture of mutual respect in an organization. When you have that, you also have an environment in which people feel valued. They feel empowered. They're quick to solve problems. They feel good about coming to work. All of their energies can go into their jobs without the loss that's siphoned off when communications impact the emotions."

I continued, "One of the sure signs that an organization is not one that values and respects people is when a supervisor, at any level, tells a subordinate to 'Leave your feelings at the door.' I heard that several times at different locations. When you think about it, psychologists would tell us that's a really dangerous admonition. The last thing we want is for people to be able to detach their being from their emotional selves. That's the kind of thing that you see in the movies when the Mafia gangsters are devoted fathers, then go out and shoot their rivals. They are caring at home but leave their emotions at the door and are cold and calculating outside the family."

"Well, that sort of thing probably only happens with gangsters and our shift supervisors. Guess we need a lot of work there." he said, trying to add some levity to the grim feedback.

"Actually, coaching at all levels would be beneficial in helping supervisors deal with subordinates appropriately. That 'Leave your feelings at the door' admonition usually means that the supervisor doesn't know how to respond, so he or she just shuts down the matter by saying that any feeling is not acceptable. An employee who is dealing with an emotional situation outside of work, such as a death, a divorce, or other trauma, may actually find work to be a welcomed diversion, but that doesn't excuse the supervisor's commands. In reality, we cannot suggest that anyone separate emotions from the logical self. Instead, we must help them to use their whole selves appropriately in the workplace and coach the supervisors on how to respond effectively," I added.

"Yes, I can see some real benefits in what you're advocating," responded the CEO.

"You'll find magic in the results of better communications. The first thing to happen is that people will feel respected and trust will begin to grow. As employees need to be less guarded and defensive, they will share more information and ideas. There will be more collaboration and cooperation in work groups and process improvement teams. You'll find that it will be easier for them to come together and pursue a common purpose. You'll find greater action between institutional knowledge and ideas coming in from outside the organization. It will be easier and safer for people to take risks, so creativity and innovation will soar," I said.

I persisted, "As Jack Welch (2005) put it, 'You need every brain in the game.' He talked about listening to employees and utilizing *all* of what they bring to the organization—their expertise, experience, energy, and potential—the whole person. Now, that doesn't mean that every suggestion must be implemented. No one expects that, but it does mean listening with respect and valuing employee commitment."

There was a long silence. Then, the CEO said slowly, "So what you're saying is that regarding people as highly as we value those multi-million dollar machines and our other property and getting good at the people stuff can have a big pay-off."

"Right, the results will be magical and that pixie dust will spill over onto your bottom line," I added. "And there'll be one more benefit. In time, you'll hear people say that they appreciate the changes in communication and relationships, not only because of the difference that it made in their work lives, but also in what happened when they used their new

As Jack Welch put it, 'You need every brain in the game' . . . *all* of what employees bring to the organization—their expertise, experience, energy, commitment, and potential— the whole person.

communication tools at home. They'll tell you stories about improved relations with children and friends. Their new skills will add to the overall quality of their lives. They will enjoy more happiness with less stress.

"It makes sense," said the CEO. " It's the kind of thing I just assumed that we were doing, but now that you describe the way we communicate and treat people, I must admit that it isn't working. We *say* that people are our most important asset, but we've got to really *live* it."

"And if people feel valued," I continued, "it changes the way they interact with one another and makes work groups function differently. Whether it's a team in the shipping department or your executive team, the work isn't impeded by big egos and turf battles. People's insecurities are not triggered and they don't become defensive; therefore, there's a huge change in what happens during your meetings. And that's the second wave of the magic wand—to change the way you meet."

The Second Wish: A New Way of Meeting

"Now that's one I like!" responded the CEO. "We spend entirely too much valuable time in meetings and we don't seem to get enough done. How would you reduce our meetings?"

"I wouldn't reduce the number of meetings that you have. I'd like to *increase* them! But before you groan, let me add that my magic wand would make your meetings more engaging, more focused, and more productive," I said.

"Well, that would require some major magic," the CEO lamented.

I continued, "You see, when people feel valued and respected, communications are open and appropriate. That sets a tone and establishes an atmosphere for free wheeling discussions. People feel comfortable expressing their ideas. Others may disagree. Then, you can have candid, open discussions and useful disagreements. People may get passionate about their ideas, and even raise their voices. It may become a heated discussion. Some people might even see it as conflict, but it really isn't. Real conflict is characterized by emotional upset. In the kinds of meetings that I'm advocating, there's lots of expression of emotion, but no one gets upset because everything and everyone can be focused on the ideas, the issues, and the content, not on each other. There's a lot of passion, but nothing is personalized or demoralizing. There is no ego involvement. Since everything is candid and in the open, there is no gossip, backbiting, political maneuvering, or behind the scenes lobbying."

I persisted, "The best part is that when decisions are made, there will be mutual support because people will reach consensus. In achieving genuine consensus, the decision makers make the *best* choice. They don't settle for the easy way out or the least objectionable choice. They don't become polarized by voting. Consensus means they fully discuss and explore the options, then make the best choice, communicate it, and support it. By the way, the use of consensus in decision making has taken a bad rap by people who just don't understand the technique or its value—but that's another discussion."

I added, "And what makes most people object to meetings is that the meetings are boring and don't seem to accomplish enough. That's usually because of not having the right people in the room or not having enough topic focus. The result is that we can't make good decisions because of the absence of appropriate people and the meandering topics deprive everyone of accomplishing what's needed. What we want is to have highly focused meetings that involve the right people. Then, the meetings will be compelling, productive, and the participants will leave with the sense that they've done something important," I continued.

"But more meetings, I don't know how that could be good," said the CEO.

"It will be very good because your meetings will accomplish more and they will be focused. You'll be making an investment in time up-front. Yes, your decision making may take more time in the beginning, but you'll save time in the long-term. You won't keep revisiting issues or correcting things after decisions have been implemented. You'll have more meetings, but no one will object because they won't last as long and you'll accomplish more than the way you're currently meeting. And even more important, people will leave the meetings with a real sense that something useful has happened and they'll know what they need to do before the next meeting. The best evidence will come when people are away and miss a meeting, they'll have the feeling that they've really *missed* something," I persisted.

"Sounds nice, but I still don't see how more meetings will improve things," protested the CEO.

"When I describe the structure and focus, you'll be able to see the results that I just outlined. That magic wand will divide your meetings into five different focuses," I continued.

The SUM

"First, there'll be the daily Stand-Up Meeting. Some people like the acronym SUM. That's where your team and you congregate around the coffee pot every morning at a certain time—let's say 8:30. You have that nice little kitchen area behind your conference room that would make a perfect rendezvous spot. You can come together promptly, and get coffee or water while everyone stands and talks. It's very casual and friendly but a good time to check-in with everyone, talk about major events of the day, get quick reminders of operational issues, and even personal topics—birthdays, whose kid won the game last night, and that sort of thing. There's no sitting or going into major issues. After 8 to 10 minutes--no more--everyone leaves and continues with their day. It gives your team an energized focus for the day. If some people need to discuss certain topics or need more time, they move into the conference room or an office and continue specific discussions without involving team members who are not relevant to their topics or issues. The reason I suggested 8:30 is I've noticed that all of your executive team seem to arrive between 7:45 and 8:00. That gives them a chance to go through voice mail, e-mail, and deal with any urgencies. The brief stand-up meeting takes place and is over before work and other meetings might begin. It's a great way to see everyone on the team, get focused, and energized for the day," I continued.

"A daily stand-up meeting. Hmm, I like that. It would give me the opportunity to see everyone informally and briefly, but every day, at least when they're in town," he reflected.

"Right, and you'll be surprised at how productive those few minutes will be every day," I concluded.

The Weekly Operational Review

"Now the second type of meeting is what you call your weekly operational review that you have every Monday afternoon," I continued.

The CEO interjected, "That's the one that everybody complains about being too long and not accomplishing enough, but I just think it's essential for us to review the weekly numbers, problems, and what's happening."

"I totally agree. That session is essential, but perhaps changing the approach to the review could eliminate the complaints and increase your meeting effectiveness. In his book, *Death by Meeting,* Patrick Lencioni (2004), advocates a weekly meeting that is highly structured but without a pre-set agenda. The reason for eliminating a predetermined agenda is that it could be outdated as soon as the meeting begins, whereas, this meeting must be relevant to immediate measures and priorities. Lencioni insisted on beginning the weekly operational meeting with sixty seconds for each team member to describe current priorities. That's followed by a review of the key business measures, such as sales, expenses, on-time shipping, inventory, cash flow, and etc. From the up-to-date metrics and each team member's priorities, a discussion can ensue of current operational issues, problem solving, and tactical obstacles. This is not a time for strategic issues, considering capital budgets, or long-term planning. Instead, it's an operational review, a time to look at what's happening in the current week, where problems might occur, and where opportunities can be expanded. This is an efficient, laser focused, 60 to 90 minute session that can be very productive. The key is in concentrating only on current issues and problems and in not being distracted by different or larger topics. Those must be saved for more appropriate meetings."

"Hmm, that focus would energize the meeting and help everyone see that we're really accomplishing something," mused the CEO.

"Right," I continued. "And since you'll be dealing with operational and immediate issues and not distracted by more complex developments, you'll be more effective in keeping everyone informed of current actions. And by following this format, you'll be able to finish the meeting in less time, so your team will stop dreading each Monday afternoon."

. . . it meets their adrenalin junkie needs to be involved in the crisis of the day.

"Yeah, I see what you mean about the magic of focused and energized," replied the CEO.

Monthly Strategic Sessions

"Whether scheduled for once or twice each month, these are longer meetings in which the larger strategic issues are brainstormed, analyzed, dissected, discussed, and decided. At the executive level, these meetings may require an entire afternoon because this is the time for discussions and decisions. Unlike the operational review, this meeting needs a carefully prepared agenda that is distributed prior to the meeting. Everyone will need time to think about and prepare for the deliberations. The agenda could include larger problems, such as why we're losing market share in a particular segment, or what it is that makes a new product line so appealing to customers. This is the time to step back and look at major issues and the long-term," I replied.

"It will definitely take some magic to get this group to put their cell phones down and think long-term," said the CEO.

"You're right about the challenge of getting some of those guys off the 'here and now' because it meets their adrenalin junkie needs to be involved in the crisis of the day; however, that's why it's so critical to teach them to be more involved with the bigger issues and what's ahead. Especially at the executive level, it's essential to be engaged in planning for the future, as well as keeping your finger on the pulse of what's happening today," I said.

There was a long silence as the CEO contemplated the resistance he would encounter in introducing more meetings and discussions that were not just about the day-to-day stuff.

I broke the quiet with, "This session could begin with lunch. You must think I put a lot of emphasis on food," I apologized. "I'm a strong advocate of nutritious food in appropriate amounts, along with snacks, such as nuts, popcorn, and raw vegetables. I can't explain why, but beginning with food gets meetings off to a casual start. Perhaps because people feel comfortable and ease into the discussion gradually, it's a productive way to begin more complex meetings, especially those with a very serious or controversial agenda," I concluded.

"Again, because of the organization's value of people and attention to communication skills, this meeting, like others, will be lively, filled with candid talk and passionate debates. Although there should be lots of disagreements, there will be no conflict because no one will experience emotional upset. All of the passion will be in the expression of ideas. There will be no bruised egos or need for turf protection," I said.

"All of that can be accomplished in an afternoon or less. I like it," concluded the CEO.

"Good," I continued, "Because you'll really make the sessions compelling when the weekly meeting is just about current operational issues, saving the bigger topics for the Monthly Strategic, and then, the Quarterly Long-Term Planning session when you have more time for in-depth probing discussions."

Quarterly Long-Term Planning

"Because of the size of your organization, the quarterly meeting will require two or three days. You'll make better decisions about the big issues in this format. It's a good time to consider, not only where we've been but, *where we're going.* This is the opportunity for careful analysis of marketing, product development, technology needs, capital expenditures, and other long-term challenges and opportunities," I said.

"But that's more emphasis on the future than we usually have," mused the CEO.

"Maybe because trying to anticipate what challenges and opportunities lie ahead can be a little scary, some people avoid or minimize strategic planning. Worse, they make it a once-a-year session or a document that sits on everyone's shelf. Yet, preparing for new products, changing trends, and future needs is critical to long-term performance. Sometimes, we can be so concerned about making a wrong prediction that we avoid adequate preparation for what's ahead. Regardless of the level of leadership, a main factor in being a successful leader is in keeping one eye clearly on the 'here and now' and the other on what's ahead," I repeated.

"That's a dizzying outlook!" quipped the CEO. "I can't disagree with what you're saying, but it's always tough to get this group into planning. I'm not sure that Bert and Chris will see the value in investing three days in planning."

"You mean on something like the J-4 expansion?" I asked. "Well, it's kind of funny when you balance three days with $400 million and something that you hope will drive one of your main products for the next several years."

"Well, when you put it that way," he replied.

"I know," I continued. "We've been conditioned to get our feelings of accomplishment from checking off those little items on our to-do lists, from working through the stuff on our desks, and from running around dealing with the crisis of the day. We have to enlarge our ideas about getting things done to include discussions, decisions, and working collaboratively with others. Today, it's not just about desk work. We have to get a sense of accomplishment from the important things, not just the routine check-offs."

"But how do we get these guys to change their mindsets and the way they've done meetings for decades?" he asked in a frustrated tone.

Now, I was becoming excited because it was clear that he was ready for a change. I jumped on the opportunity and continued with, "We can outline how you'll introduce the SUM and the changes in your weekly operations review. At first, you'll have to make a phone call or two, issue reminders, or even prod one or two to participate in the daily stand-up. Because of the informality, some people may regard participation as an option, but when they see that you're committed, and they begin to enjoy benefits of the quick daily contacts with everyone, they'll be there every day that they're in town and it will become an important part of their daily routine. Adding structure to your weekly meetings will energize the group and make them open to other changes," I added.

"I'm pretty good at running meetings, but I don't know that I want to take on several days of trying to herd these guys through the planning process. And besides, it's frustrating to have to run the meeting and participate at the same time," he complained.

"It will be more productive if you have a skilled facilitator from the outside for your longer or complex meetings," I said. "Having someone who can guide the topics and manage the environment will allow you to relax and focus on the subject. And these kinds of meetings have unique requirements. For example, this upcoming quarterly strategic planning required considerable preparation from all of the participants. And since the topic requires long sessions without interruptions or distractions, it's usually best to have them off site—like today's session. Of course, a conference center, like we're using for today's meeting is always a great choice, but if you need to cut costs, you could take your team to the Monroe location where you have a very nice meeting facility. There are lots of ways of arranging the session, but it must be well planned and without distractions. Video, white boards, flip charts, and technology for projecting presentations are often useful, but I usually describe the three essentials for a productive meeting as:

- freedom from distractions
- comfortable chairs
- good food

If you have those basics, you're off to a successful beginning."

"You should have told me about the three essentials before we booked this conference center," he joked.

"Well, you're providing quiet and comfort in an exceptional atmosphere, so that's insurance for a successful Long-Term Planning Session. And this will be a perfect example of what I'm advocating. For instance, we've carefully surveyed the seven participants and included their priorities and concerns in the agenda. We'll be talking about your new marketing initiatives, the opportunities in Asia, and your global business. It's a highly focused and relevant agenda but it will move along and be very energizing," I said.

Quarterly Team Building

"The fifth type of meeting is the most often neglected . . ."

"You mean there's yet another kind of meeting in that magic wand?" he interrupted.

"Well, yes, and this is probably the most often neglected function because it's easy to say that everyone gets along just fine or there's just no time or budget for building the team," I responded.

"Oh, you mean the touchy-feely stuff," laughed the CEO.

"No, I mean the trust, relationship, and common purpose stuff," I retorted with a smile. "Team building is another of those processes that has gotten a bad reputation because people have used it as an excuse for all kinds of activities. But team building is about enhancing relationships. We can't expect people to work cohesively and collaboratively if we don't start with effective relationships. Now, I don't mean that everyone has to be socially glued together or buddy-buddy. But it's essential for the relations to be sufficiently comfortable for people to express ideas, disagree, and make good decisions. And people have to build trust and credibility with each other." I laughed, "One of your account managers told me that the downside of being promoted and having to relocate from Macyville to Chicago was trying to find a good dentist and a reliable plumber. In the big city, he didn't have trusting relationships with people who could give him reliable recommendations. We depend on relationships for so much. Mark told me that 90% of your sales were relationship based, and yet, it's so hard to get people to see the need for paying attention to building relationships, and especially any activity that is intended to enhance relations."

For an activity to contribute to team building, what happens must enhance and be related to day-to-day team interactions.

"You sound a bit frustrated. Is it tough to get people to take time for the touch-feely stuff?" the CEO teased.

"It's the reluctance to deal with anything that might be fun, related to emotions, or not purely fact and data based, I guess. Maybe it's the fear of being vulnerable or exposed," I admitted.

"I understand that the goal is cohesiveness, but can't we deal with the relationship stuff and build the teamwork in a way that feels safe and comfortable?" he asked.

"Absolutely! I responded. "The team building that I'm advocating can actually take place at various times or be combined with your quarterly long-term planning session as we're doing today. All we need to do is to structure the session with some time for attention to the relationships, for considering how effective decisions are made, and for building the bond that facilitates having a mutual purpose to energize the high performance goals. For example, in this meeting, we scheduled the arrival to include dinner and an evening activity that will be enjoyable but allow plenty of time for informal conversation. Having all of our meals together will help

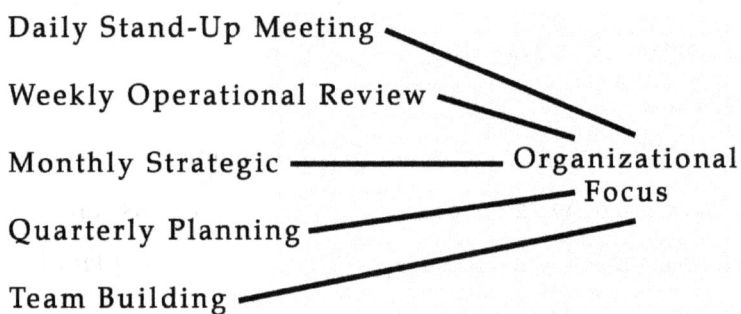

Daily Stand-Up Meeting

Weekly Operational Review

Monthly Strategic —————— Organizational
                                    Focus
Quarterly Planning

Team Building

to maintain the flow and encourage lots of team interaction. Before we begin the main discussion tomorrow morning, we'll have a *content free* activity in which we'll analyze the team's decision process. Then, when we get to the real discussions, you'll have a structure to reflect upon and a learning experience with which to assess the real process. On Thursday, we'll include another process activity, something that helps people know each other at a deeper, useful level for collaboration. Those activities will be especially helpful to Joe, since he's only been a part of your team for about seven months. Then, we'll end the session with the whole group on the lake," I reminded him. "There are many facets to team building," I continued.

"The team activity, or what you actually do isn't terribly important. What matters is that it has direct relationship to the team, along with relevance to the team's work and how they interact. All too often, people go rafting or through a ropes course, but it's just enjoyable recreation. For an activity to contribute to team building, what happens in the activity must enhance and be related to day-to-day team interactions.

That's why it's worth the expense to have these types of meetings managed by a skilled facilitator."

"That would be you," quipped the CEO.

"Yes," I admitted. "You were very wise to bring me along to manage the dynamics and maintain the focus. I have the same objectives as the team." Then I added, "The one caution is that you don't include anyone else except your team members in these sessions. If you choose to hold these planning and team sessions in attractive off-site locations, you may have suggestions of including spouses and others. There's only one response: Don't do it! Except for a neutral facilitator, the presence of just one other person can change the dynamics. Even if others are not present at all of the meetings, just being on-site, being seen at dinner and passed in the hall, impacts the atmosphere."

"Oh, so you're saying that we shouldn't bring spouses or managers, but it's okay that we're including you in this session," he laughed.

"Right, I quickly replied. "If I were a guest, my agenda would be more personal—perhaps to enjoy the scenery, the pool, the spa, the food, and . . ."

"I get the point," interrupted the CEO, "It's all about maintaining the focus."

"Right," I responded, "So to summarize, what we've been discussing has been about your meetings with the executive team, but what I'm advocating is adaptable at any level in the organization."

"Uhh, you want me to bring the shipping teams to Lake Tahoe?" asked the CEO.

"It would be nice, and I'm certain they would enjoy it" I laughed, "But the key word was *adapted,*" I clarified. "For example, at the beginning of their shift, your department teams or shipping teams could have the daily three to five minute stand-up meeting in which they discuss the priorities and other relevant topics for the day. Each week, they could have a 15 to 20 minute operations review in which they look at their safety, productivity, quality, and other metrics, and talk about how they can increase their key measures. Each month, they can have a 30-45 minute strategy or problem-solving meeting in which they bring together ideas for solving technical glitches, team concerns, and other issues. Although you may not be able to take hourly employees off-site, you could begin their meetings with snacks or beverages. And you might be surprised at how cost effective team training can be for hourly employees."

I continued, "Also, it's very effective to bring all of the employees in a department or in the facility together for a short quarterly update where everyone can hear from managers about the state of the industry, the business, and a general description of how things are going. Don't make your employees find out about your organization from the news medis or an online search. Instead, keep them informed just as you do other stakeholders. It's easy to assume that the clerk in the mailroom or the guy driving the lift truck isn't interested in the business or can't understand it. And certainly, that may be true for a few people, but it's amazing how much interest hourly employees have in the overall organization.   Sharing that information is a small price for increasing their loyalty and trust," I said.

"Well, we try to do that now at our annual employee dinners, but I see what you mean about the impact of having shorter and more frequent meetings with them," he said.

"True," I responded. "You'll gain incredible momentum from honest, candid conversation in these meetings."

"I like the idea of having each meeting highly focused," he continued.

"The structure I just described may not cover every topic or every issue that might arise, but the skills that everyone will acquire will make it easy to setup special meetings. And the good thing is that no one will complain because they know that everything will be focused and it will be a good use of their time. You know, meetings are an integral part of leadership, especially in a collaborative team environment. Meetings are part of the job!" I concluded.

"Yeah, well maybe this will make them a better part of the job," he said.

"And the best part," I continued, "is when you see that the practice of daily, weekly operational, monthly strategic, team building, and long-term planning meetings can be adapted to fit the world and space of any group in your organization. And because these

It isn't logical, but taking out time for focused effective meetings and interactions can actually add to productivity.

meetings are characterized by value for people, productive communication skills, and effective meeting structures, everyone is excited about what takes place. They like the information they gain, and the overall results. And while some critics might see this as a loss of valuable time away from the job, that isn't what happens. Because of the energized atmosphere, all of the measures increase, even productivity. So while you're taking time away for meetings, you're gaining the time usually lost for gossip and distractions because the real information is flowing freely. You're also adding effectiveness through having everyone know what the priorities are and what's happening. Most of all, you'll increase employee loyalty because everyone will have a better idea of what's occurring in the larger organization and feel a greater part of things," I said.

I confessed, "I know it's hard to believe that taking time away from productivity for meetings actually saves time, but everywhere I've seen this practiced, production, employee satisfaction, and other measure-ables increase. It isn't logical, but taking out time for interactions and focused effective meetings can actually add to productivity measures. The information sharing and empowerment energize the workforce and increase results at every level."

After a long silence, the CEO concluded, "Maybe we should have had this discussion prior to planning this off-site."

"No, it's never too late to begin meeting effectively. When people are valued as assets and meetings are structured and focused, the sessions are compelling and productive. You'll find that people will stop dreading meetings. This session will be a great example of what I just described," I promised. "Now, are you ready for my third wish?" I asked.

"Yes, but there's the lodge up ahead, so hold onto that thought until we're set up in the conference center," he said.

"Actually, the timing is okay because I could really use a white board or something to diagram the third wish. Since we'll have a couple of hours before the others arrive, I'll check out the conference room and we can continue the discussion when you're ready," I replied.

The Third Wish: The Scope of Work

After confirming that all of the necessary materials and equipment were in place, the CEO and I sat down at the end of the conference table.

"You know, Z, your two ideas about people as assets and meeting effectiveness have me intrigued. How can you have a third idea with as much potential as those two?"

"Oh, my third wish is to significantly change the *way* that people work in organizations," I said with glee.

"And just how and why would you want to do that?" chuckled the CEO.

"I've noticed how often employees find themselves off-track when they do things without getting the right people involved or without getting permission or buy-in for their actions. At the same time, I've observed how many opportunities are missed when people hesitate to engage. It's as if they're waiting for a formal invitation. If we could clearly define the areas where people are free to work independently, where they need to accomplish tasks while keeping key people informed, when they need to engage and involve others, and where they must

. . . many opportunities are missed when people hesitate to engage. It's as if they're waiting for a formal invitation.

not act without specific formal permission, everyone could be incredibly more productive, creative, and feel more confident and secure, I said".

"I don't quite get it. What I hear is that you want to clearly define each individual's scope of the involvement of others. I guess you mean the boss and the coworkers." clarified the CEO.

"Right," I said.

"But that sounds way too cumbersome for me, and probably for most managers," responded the CEO.

"That's because I'm not doing a good job of describing the structure," I said. "I can probably sketch it out on the white board and make a clearer picture," I added.

"Think of these as a stack of blocks," I said as I drew a large black rectangle on the white board. "This represents all of the tasks, the work, and the stuff, that you expect an employee at any level to do," as I wrote *independent* inside of the large block. "This represents all of his or her individual performance and accomplishments, the things that you expect the person to do independently. The supervisor and others don't

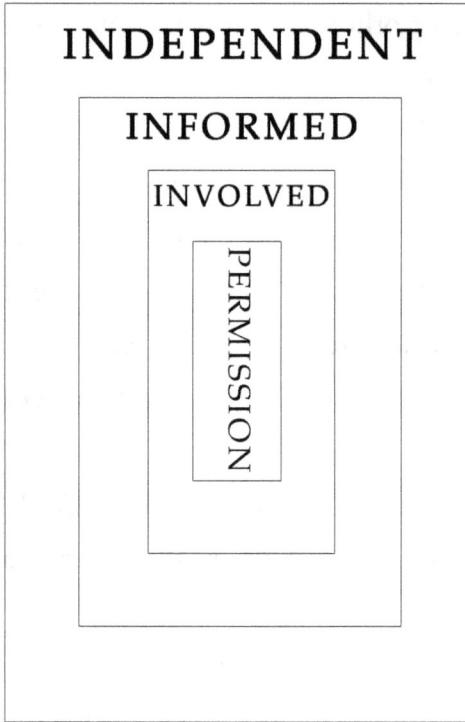

need to be engaged. Instead, the person just does the tasks and is accountable for the performance."

"Okay," said the CEO, "but being able to work with others is important in many jobs."

"Yes, and that work falls into two areas. This part is represented by the next block that I'm stacking on top of *independent*. We'll call the second block, *informed*. It represents a second kind of work that most of us need to do. We perform the tasks, somewhat independently but while keeping others informed of what we're doing, our progress, and its impact. We need to do the work, but keep the key stakeholders and/or supervisors informed. They don't need to be engaged in what we're doing, but they need to know what's going on. Actually, knowing what we're doing can help them to do their jobs." I added.

"Yeah," said the CEO, "But a lot of people don't like having to report-in."

"And that's unfortunate," I responded, "I guess that inflated egos or power mongers just need to feel in charge of everything and can't deal with sharing information. But keeping others informed isn't about reporting-in, being submissive, or subservient. Instead,

Keeping others informed isn't about reporting-in, being submissive, or subservient... It's about being effective.

keeping others 'in the know' is about being collaborative and part of the team. It's about being more effective."

I continued, "One of the tools that I like to give ambitious young employees is the practice of a brief weekly update that they give their supervisors, either verbally or via e-mail. It's a simple, concise overview of current work projects, what's anticipated, and any barriers or resources that they need. Whether it's a 15-minute conversation, a one-page bullet list, or a concise e-mail, I've never encountered a boss who disliked the practice. Of course, we're not talking about inundating the supervisor with information or being dependent on others. Instead, it's sharing appropriate information and stimulating overall effectiveness."

"I can relate to that one," said the CEO. "If you asked me to list the best performers I've seen in my career, the names would be the same as for sharing information, but those people are too rare. Take Dennis, for example."

"Who? I don't believe I've met . . ." I said

"No, he retired last year," interjected the CEO, "So you wouldn't have met him. But Dennis would have been the best operations guy I ever saw except that you constantly had to pry information out of him. Working with Dennis was always frustrating because he resisted being open with information and operated on what he called a 'need to know' basis. The problem was that it was all about *his* perception of need. Working with him was always exasperating because I so often found myself in the dark or found out about things at the last minute. Yeah, Dennis could have been good, but . . ."

He looked away, paused for a long moment, and then said, "Now, I'm following you,"

I continued. "You'll notice that this third block is smaller because it represents less of the typical employee's total work, but it's certainly not less important," "It represents *involved,* the kinds of projects and work that require synergy, interactions, team members, or the supervisor—a high degree of interaction with others. Although the individual may perform some tasks independently, at the same time the involvement of others may be required to accomplish the whole project."

"Like this meeting for strategic planning," said the CEO. "It would be crazy for me or any one person to undertake corporate planning alone."

"Now, we've got the picture. Process improvements, major projects, or solving complex problems need the involvement of people with diverse expertise, experience, and approaches. No matter whether it's at executive level or at the hourly employee level, you won't keep solving the same problems or dealing with the same undesirable results if the relevant people are involved. And having them engaged in the preparation stage, the problem solving, or whatever it is can make a huge difference in the implementation phase. Remember that adage, 'People tend to support that which they've helped to create.' So, involvement is the key. What I'm trying to describe is how complex work requires a kind of dance that includes some solos, or independent work, along with some carefully choreographed performance in which there are intricate and well coordinated maneuvers in concert with other relevant people!" I exclaimed.

"Ah, we've got an interesting picture here—this dance of working with others," mused the CEO.

"Yeah, more and more of today's success is about the ability to develop relationships and work collaboratively. The days of the *Lone Ranger* belong to the 1950's," I added.

"We certainly agree on that one!" said the CEO.

I continued, "And finally, this very small block on top represents *permission.* These are the kinds of things for which an employee must gain specific, usually formal, authorization before acting. For example, in most organizations, you wouldn't want anyone to make any changes that impact the legal stuff, such as contracts and state or federal requirements, without getting permission from the highest level or legal authority in the organization, right?" I asked.

"Well, of course," replied the CEO.

"And you don't want anyone to even think about changing any company policies, such as personnel or expense policies, right?" I asked.

The CEO nodded.

"And what about expenditures? I'll guess that you don't allow an hourly employee to spend any company money without specific permission, but the amount probably increases with level of responsibility. Your Greenville manager might spend $10,000 without permission from a vice president, while you can probably spend a little more without getting board approval, right?" I asked.

"Sure, but we're not that rigid about other things," protested the CEO.

"Right," I replied. "The key is in knowing exactly what requires permission, when to inform or involve others, and where people can act independently. Although there are plenty of examples of employees who get into trouble and do things they shouldn't, a more common problem is that people hesitate to act for fear of getting into trouble with someone, especially the boss. They're waiting for that formal invitation to perform."

I continued, "The other typical mistake is assuming that they must ask, 'Mother, may I?' when actually, they just need to do the work and keep the relevant people informed of their actions. People can become frustrated or angry because they confuse the need to inform others with the necessity of obtaining permission. It's easy to overlook how much others gain from well-coordinated communications. Employees' confidence can really be increased when they completely grasp that keeping the boss or colleagues informed is not about their own lack of power but about helping others do their jobs better. Keeping the boss and others informed isn't about power, it's about being effective. One of the best ways to help people feel empowered is to carefully outline how few areas really require formal permission. Knowing the specific permission requirements, and how rare they really are, can be illuminating and help us to realize just how much freedom we have to do the work that we love."

"But come on, don't you think 99% of people actually know what you've just described?" asked the CEO.

"Some people have learned, through observation and making mistakes, where to work independently, when to inform or involve others, and when to seek permission; however, it isn't obvious to everyone or transparent in every organization. A good example in your organization would be Max. You've described him as micromanaging his subordinates but keeping you in the dark or isolated from issues or situations that you really should know about. Remember how angry you were last October when you accidentally heard from a vendor that he had decided to scale back your Blackwell operation?"

"Okay, now that you put it that way, I guess that learning those four areas could benefit all of us and at every level," the CEO said slowly.

"Yes, clarification and effective communication always benefit interactions in any organization. And clarifying the scope of everyone's work adds such security and self-confidence. It becomes very empowering," I added.

"Your magic is all about the 'people stuff' isn't it?" replied the CEO. "Don't you want to change any of our product lines, our technology, or our financials?

"That won't be necessary," I said. "When you value the people, it creates an atmosphere of trust, respect, good communications, and positive relationships. In turn, that can help to change the way that you meet and the results of your collaborative efforts. As everyone understands the expectations, when to inform, when to involve, when to get permission, and when to work independently, all of those other things that you mentioned will be the results. It changes the workplace for everyone. It makes all of your jobs and your stock options more secure because it makes the organization stronger and the company more profitable."

"Now, that would be a great magic trick!" concluded the CEO.

The Alchemy

It was exhilarating to walk out onto the balcony and gaze at the incredible scenery of Lake Tahoe, but what really energized the group was the laser-like focus and unified direction that the CEO and his team were able to achieve in their sessions. The discussions and activities seemed to give them a cohesion that they had not experienced before. As with any off-site, the total value of the session could not be known until the participants returned to their everyday work. For this group, the newly created teamwork and direction really seemed magical. Happily, the CEO wanted a commitment from me to facilitate future off-site sessions and continue the work in individual and organization development.

Although it was tempting to allow the Lake Tahoe group to believe that their new accomplishments were due to my involvement, I had to point to their actions. In time, they developed a highly focused and successful

When you value people, it creates an atmosphere of trust, respect, good communications, and positive relationships.

organization that began with new ways of meeting, defining their scope of work, and the new culture of trust and respect from valuing people as assets. I could take little credit for their achievement, but I quietly enjoyed tons of gratification in seeing their increased job satisfaction and tremendous successes.

Positive Results for the Organization

Gravity dictates that buildings are constructed from the bottom up. Unlike buildings, organizations are built from the top down because they are governed by the principles of human psychology, not physics. Whatever the product, size, governance, or finances, all organizations begin with humans. It's the human at the top of the organization in the leader role who begins the process of organizational change. Even though it is possible for others to influence parts of the organizational culture, it is the leader who has the greatest influence on the overall culture. When the leader acknowledges people's needs and capitalizes on ways to enable employees to work effectively, the impact is swift and large.

. . . buildings are built from the bottom up.

. . . organizations are built from the top down.

It's so easy when everyone experiences the better environment. Subtle changes in the culture result in marked improvements in organizational success. These changes produce all kinds of process and product improvements. People become careful with managing money and controlling costs. Even the lowest level employees feel valued and understand their contribution and responsibilities to the whole. Better relationships contribute to better decisions. Most of all, as the egos, politics, and turf protection disappear, amazing gains occur everywhere. It's just magical to accomplish enormous organizational change by making three very low cost improvements.

Jeff and his co-workers at the technology company came to enjoy the same success that I've seen develop in other organizations when these fundamentals become a part of the infrastructure. Although each organization has its own uniqueness, the three wishes can greatly enhance chances for success. Leaders and organizations that place a special value on employee well-being gain a double pay-off. They get the benefit of having a satisfied, highly engaged, strong performing workforce.

In addition, they gain the financial productivity of that workforce.

Positive Results for the Individual

Although published in 1911, Frederick Taylor's ideas that only managers gain satisfaction from work still plague us in the twenty-first century. Taylor's fixation on efficiency led to his overlooking that, regardless of rank or tasks, it is possible for anyone to enjoy what they do. Today's employees invest far too much of their lives at work not to enjoy what they are doing. People usually report a higher sense of job satisfaction when they work in environments in which they believe that they are important and what they do is important.

When barriers to good performance are removed, frustration and dissatisfaction are diminished; therefore, people have a greater positive regard for their workplace. Working under less stress and with more satisfaction leads to a better quality of work life. Knowing when to get permission, when to inform or involve, and when to work independently reduces the fear of making a mistake or getting into trouble. When the fear is removed, the desire to do a good job will be increased.

Contrary to Frederick Taylor's belief, in today's world, people want to experience achievement, enjoyment, and intrinsic reward from work. If what they perceive as their basic needs are being met, then just a pay-check is not usually enough. Too often, however, when people can't find the satisfaction that they want, they look for a better environment elsewhere. Certainly, if you're in a negative or hostile work environment, the obvious solution is to get out quickly. A more common situation is that things are not simply black and white. There are some aspects of the job that you like or want to keep while there are other annoying circumstances that you want to change. If that's your situation, concentrate on what's good about your workplace and use some of the ideas from my magic wand to improve the less desirable parts of your job. If it doesn't seem possible to change the negatives, see if they're out weighed by the positive aspects. Just like people, no job is perfect, but we can enhance the assets and de-emphasize the liabilities.

Look at what you can change and what the rewards will be for your change. You might have to give up complaining about your job, but that would be a small price to pay for getting more enjoyment from what you do and where you invest so much of your life.

Changing others isn't as easy as changing yourself. Sometimes, coaxing people to improve the ways that they've done things for decades seems impossible. That's when it helps to have support from leadership. Perhaps leadership is the reason that the Lake Tahoe group had so much success. Their CEO was committed, but even if you aren't the CEO or at the top of the organization, you can make a difference in your workplace. You may not be able to change the whole organization, but you can change *you* and your corner of the workplace. Begin with some ideas from the following lists:

Value People as Assets

- Express your value for and appreciation of others.

- Thank others when they are helpful to you.

- Smile and express interest in other people.

- When appropriate, demonstrate support for the ideas and contributions of others.

- Celebrate others' accomplishments and successes.

- Communicate with respect.

- Monitor your communications. Be specific, positive, non-defensive, and avoid the gossip.

- Trust others and be trustworthy.

- Assume that colleagues will do the right thing until you have contrary evidence.

- Don't meet your own power and ego needs at the expense of others.

- Develop appropriate work relationships, not social or personal, but collegial team relations.

Make Meetings Focused and Effective

- Manage your own behavior in meetings and be an example of professionalism.

- Be prepared and punctual for meetings.

- Stay on the topic, avoid inappropriate digressions or comments that might encourage others to stray.

- Listen and let others know that you're listening by giving them eye contact and your careful attention.

- Encourage others to participate. Seek their ideas, opinions, and input.

- Ask questions, clarify, and build on the ideas of others.

- Diplomatically discourage attention seeking behavior, inappropriate joking, and discussions that divert time and energy from the important issues.

- Foster meeting structures that focus on daily, operational, strategic, and team issues.

Define the Scope of Your Work

- Be an independent, strong performer.

- Be dependable, reliable, and accountable for your actions.

- Share appropriate information with relevant people.

- Involve the right people in projects—colleagues with the expertise, information, and abilities to be a strong part of the team.

- Determine exactly what you can and can't do without permission and confirm with your supervisor.

- Be proactive and don't wait for an invitation.

- Keep the boss informed through a weekly 15-minute *update* conversation or a bullet list that you send via e-mail about current issues and progress, what you anticipate, and any resources or support that you need. Make it a concise overview of present activities, future work, and possible needs.

Your ideas for improving your workplace

•

•

•

•

•

•

•

•

•

•

•

•

•

•

•

•

•

•

•

When you regard coworkers as assets, enhance your communication skills, demonstrate effective behaviors in meetings, and define the scope of your work, you may be surprised by the personal satisfaction that you'll enjoy. Others will likely become interested in the changes they see. You'll find that your new behaviors and skills will be contagious.

Allow me to lend you my magic wand so that you can make a difference in your workplace, and in the process, enhance your own success and the quality of your work life.

Abracadabra!

References

Lencioni, P. (2004). *Death by Meeting*. San Francisco: Jossey Bass.

Taylor, F.W. (1911/2007) *Principles of Scientific Management*. New York: BiblioBazaar.

Welch, J. (2005). *Winning*. New York: Harper Collins.

For more magic

and additional ideas go to

www.drzelma.com